# THE INDIAN AND HIS PUEBLO

by LOUISE LEE FLOETHE

with pictures by

RICHARD FLOETHE

Text copyright © 1960 Louise Lee Floethe
Pictures copyright © 1960 Richard Floethe
All rights reserved
Printed in the United States of America

CHARLES SCRIBNER'S SONS New York

# THE INDIAN AND HIS PUEBLO

This is the story of the Indian and his pueblo. Pueblo is the Spanish word for village. In the early days when the Spaniards were exploring they gave the Indian villages this name. And they called the people of the village Pueblo Indians.

This pueblo is close to the Rio Grande in New Mexico. It is on the great sweeping mesa. In the distance are mountains, deep blue against a bright blue sky. Rounded hills dotted with piñon and juniper trees guard the pueblo. It is a land of bright sunlight and of shadow. It is a dry land where rain is scarce and drought is a constant danger.

Long ago the Indian learned the best way to live in this land. That is why we still find many of the old ways in the pueblos today.

The houses have always been built of a mixture of clay and sand called adobe. The Indian did not need to look far for adobe. It was in the earth. It was part of the bare, dry country in which he made his home. When the Spaniards came to explore they taught the Indian how to make adobe into bricks by pouring it into wooden molds and drying it in the hot sun. Now adobe bricks are used by the Pueblo people for most of their houses.

After the adobe house is lived in for a while it begins to crumble. But it is simple enough to patch it up with more adobe. It is the woman's work to plaster the house walls.

The Indian woman works hard. She keeps her house neat and clean. She cares for her children. She grinds corn at her mealing bin. She dries meat, vegetables and fruit. She keeps the fire going. She cooks all the family's food.

"Busy, busy, busy," she says. "Never a moment to be idle."

The Pueblo woman bakes bread in a beehive oven outside her house.

The woman makes a fire on the oven floor and lets it burn, tightly closed, for hours. When the oven is heated she sweeps the ashes from the oven and puts in the bread to bake.

The making of pottery is woman's work.

For the bottom of the bowl she pats out a flat round piece of clay. Then she rolls a small piece of clay between her hands until she makes a coil long enough to fit around the flat bottom. She places more and more coils, one on top of another, until her bowl is as high as she wants it. Then she dips her fingers in water and smoothes the bowl inside and out. After that she takes a polished stone and smoothes the bowl again.

After the bowls are dried the decoration is painted on. Then the pottery is ready for the fire. The bowls are put upside down on a grate and covered with cakes of dried dung. The dung is the fuel. When the pottery is taken from the fire it is strong and beautiful.

The Indian man has many jobs to do. He hunts. He farms. He takes care of the animals. He gathers wood for the fire.

When spring comes the Indian man is very busy. Old grass must be burned off the fields. The irrigation ditches must be cleaned for they hold the water which brings life to the crops. All the men of the pueblo help with the ditches.

Early in the morning the men leave the pueblo with shovels over their shoulders. They dig all day. They laugh and sing as they work. When the ditches are clean they are ready for the spring flow of water from the river.

The most important Indian crop is corn. But the Indian also grows other things. He grows squash, pumpkins, melons and beans.

Long ago the Indian learned how to get the best from his dry soil. He did not plow. He left the crusty cover of the earth untouched to protect the dampness underneath. He planted his seed deep so the roots of the plants could reach the dampness. His corn made long roots and short, tough leaves. It grew in thick clumps. Even if the wind blew hard the corn in the center of the clumps did not tear.

In olden times the Pueblo farmer used tools made of wood. Later he learned to use the white man's tools. The Indian farmer has always had to work very hard to get a good crop.

Long ago it was man's work to do the weaving. He wove beautiful fabrics made of cotton. Later, when the Spaniards came, he learned to weave with wool. He used a loom made of two upright poles and two cross bars holding the warp frame. The weaver worked from the bottom up. He wove very fast. The blankets he made were strong and warm.

But today the Pueblo Indian no longer weaves. He buys his clothes, just as we do, at the store. Often he buys his blankets from his neighbor the Navajo Indian.

Children of the pueblo love to play, like children everywhere. They have many games. One of the favorites is shinny. It is played with a curved stick and a ball made of stuffed deerskin. The boys run fast and drive the ball with their sticks. But they do not try to reach a goal.

Little girls like to build playhouses. Often they have dolls made of wood or corn husks.

In olden times boys learned the work of the pueblo from their fathers. Girls learned the work of the house from their mothers. Today boys and girls of the pueblo go to school. The children speak their own Indian language at home and English in school.

Dancing is an important part of pueblo life. There are many kinds of dances. On the next page is a corn dance.

In the plaza is a round building with steps going up to the roof entrance. This is the kiva.

No white man may enter the kiva.

Inside the kiva the Indian men meet to think about the ways of their religion. They sing songs which they believe help to ripen the corn and to bring good crops. They plan dances. There are dances to help the hunt, the spring planting or to bring rain.

Inside the kiva the men also talk about how to live a good life. They are told not to quarrel. To be generous. To welcome others to their homes. To be helpful. The meetings in the kiva are happy times. Women bring food. The men laugh and joke with one another. In the old days the men liked going to the meetings in the kiva. They still do today.

On Sundays the Indians go to church. The big bell in the steeple rings out through the pueblo and calls them to prayer.

Winter is the time for the Buffalo Dance.

The Indian believes that the Buffalo Dance will help him with his hunting.

The Indian says, "If, when we dance, our hearts are right, the hunt will be good."

When there is a rabbit hunt all the men of the pueblo take part. They divide in two long lines surrounding a large part of country. Very slowly they come together driving the rabbits ahead of them. When they are near enough they kill the rabbits by throwing the rabbit stick, a flat, slightly curved piece of wood which can be thrown quite a distance.

All the people are happy if the hunt is a success. Then everyone will have meat to eat in the pueblo.

Many changes have come to the pueblo. Some houses now have electricity, radios and television. Some have running water. The people have cars in which to drive to work. They buy clothes from the store. Children learn new ways in school.

Yet the old life of the pueblo still goes on. Long ago the Indian decided upon a good way of life. Now some of the unimportant things like clothing and ways of travel have been changed. But the old laws and beliefs go on.